Cover image provided by Robert Lyn Nelson.
Feature photos by Leah Latini.
© 2011 Fit to Go, All Rights Reserved under the Standard United States Copyright Agreement.

Contact Tina by email Tina@FittoGoByTina.com
www.FitToGoByTina.com

ISBN 978-1-257-84677-1

This book is not intended to cure any medical conditions. Please consult your doctor for any medical advice, and before you decide to follow a meal plan.

This book may not be reproduced in whole or in part, in any form or by any means, electronic or mechanical, including photocopying, recording, or by any information storage and retrieval system now known or hereafter invented, without written permission from the author.

Recipes by Tina Richards

This book is dedicated to Gary, my amazing husband of 21 years; my best friend.

Also to the love of our lives "Rajah". Our loyal Arctic Wolf, "We will see you in heaven."

Index

MY STORY 1

SESAME GINGER CHICKEN 4

STUFFED GARLIC HERB BURGER 7

MANGO SALMON & SIDES 9

ARTICHOKE PESTO PASTA 13

BLACK OLIVE PESTO PASTA 14

ARTICHOKE FLANK STEAK 16

SHOPPING GUIDE & MORE SIDES 18

My Story

Growing up in Southern California, fitness and healthy living have always been a big part of my life. From a young age I was busy with physical activities, like skiing the local mountain, and competitively showing my horse throughout high school.

I took this love of healthy living and went off to college full of enthusiasm. I was ready to learn all that I could about nutrition and business in an effort to turn my passion into a career. I won a local tennis event and local 10k, shortly after moving to Newport Beach. My body was at it's peak performance and still running largely on youth!

As it turns out, I was never taught the importance of nutritional supplements, and eventually age snuck up on me. Suddenly at 36 years old, I found myself sick with an immune issue. I was shocked that I could be vulnerable to such serious conditions. I was convinced that I must be missing something and set out looking for a solution.

I embarked on this quest for answers and was blessed to find a man named Thomas T. Tierney, C.N.S., who introduced me to a revolutionary line of raw sourced, chemical-free products. By sticking to a regime of healthy eating, regular exercise, and supplements, I was able to regain my strength and become active again.

With my genuine excitement and powerful personal story, I was able to build a successful business helping others nurture their bodies though food, high quality supplements, and exercise. Then, finally after 6 years, decided to make a major life change and set off for my next great adventure.

It was at this point that my husband and I moved to Aspen, Colorado, where I began working as a chef at a children's ski school and exploring my passion for health through food. Besides all of the amazing changes that were happening to my career life, we also found and adopted our newest family member, Rajah, an Arctic Wolf. I also stepped up my culinary skills by taking a few gourmet cooking classes, and my creativity began to flourish. Life was good.

After 7 years of life in Aspen, my husband and I decided to come home to Southern California. Shortly after, I began working at an exquisite home and cooking shop in San Clemente called "Villa Cucina".

I soon became known for my healthy, creative cooking, and friends and clients alike began asking me for recipes they could use in their everyday lives.

I could see that life was pushing me in this new direction, and my love of cooking only continued to grow the more that I learned.

I utilized many of the gourmet seasoning mixes, sauces, and marinades to create unique recipes that are full of flavor! My new creations were a huge hit, and I knew I had struck a chord with the busy working families that wanted to create healthy, tasty meals on the go.

My need for convenience in the kitchen only increased when my husband and I decided to live full-time on our sailboat in early 2009.

I currently teach fitness boot camps in the harbor and offer cooking classes to small groups on our sailboat. Part of the concept being, if I can make amazing healthy meals while living on a boat… anyone can do it!

It is with this spirit of empowerment and joy, that I present my first cookbook to the world. The recipes found in this book are all full of flavor, while still being healthy. They are also designed to fit into your busy lifestyle by utilizing a small number of core ingredients (see the "Shopping Guide" at the end of the book for more tips on shopping for premium ingredients).

I hope that you will enjoy my recipes as much as my family and friends have!

There will be more to come!

Tina Richards

Sesame Ginger Chicken

Who doesn't love the delicious flavors of Asian cooking? Unfortunately, many Asian-inspired dishes often have high sugar content, making it a no-no if you're trying to stay lean.

In this recipe, we use fresh oranges and a good quality marinade to pack an intense flavor punch without the sugar!

Ingredients
(serves 2)
2 Chicken Breasts
Sesame Ginger Dressing Lite
(Paul Newman's Brand)
Lite Soy Sauce
1 Fresh Orange
1 TB Yogurt Butter
(Brummel & Brown)

In a 1 gal. plastic locking bag pour 2 cups of salad dressing and 1/4 cup lite soy sauce. Cut orange in half, squeeze the juice of one-half into the bag, and save the other half for later. Place fat-trimmed chicken breasts into marinade and seal the bag. Then, place bag into the refrigerator to marinate for 1 hour.

In a medium saute pan, heat Brummel & Brown Yogurt Butter. Once butter has melted, gently place chicken breasts into pan. Also add 1 TB of the marinade to sear in extra flavor.

Saute chicken for 4 minutes on each side. Then slice 2 thin pieces of orange and lay them over chicken breasts. Squeeze the juice of the remaining orange over chicken and continue to saute until meat is cooked through.

SIDES: Serve chicken with Cinnamon Sweet Potato and Sauteed Green Beans with Almonds. *(See page 22 for additional side recipes.)*

Our water dog "Sushi" waiting for leftovers!

Stuffed Garlic Herb Burger

Ingredients *(serves 2)*
1/2 lb Ground Turkey
1/2 lb Ground Beef
1 Brown Egg *(Organic)*
Wind & Willow Garlic Herb (Cheeseball Mix)
Fresh Parmesan Cheese
Dried Parsley
Lite Cream Cheese
1 TB Yogurt Butter (Brummel & Brown)
1 Cup Porcini
1 Whole Garlic
Fisherman's Wharf Seasoning

Yes, we have a grill on a boat! Grilling is a key element in any healthy lifestyle. When you grill food, you can infuse an intense amount of flavor without all the fat.

Hint: We always serve burgers without the bun to cut down on needless carbohydrates.

Make cheeseball mix as directed and place in refrigerator to chill. *(You may replace regular cream cheese with Tofutti brand cream cheese, and replace regular butter with Brummel & Brown Yogurt Butter to reduce calories).*

In a small sauté pan, heat 1 TB yogurt butter and sauté 3-4 cloves of garlic. Add porcini mushrooms to garlic and butter, then a dash of Fisherman's Wharf Seasoning. Sauté until mushrooms are browned; chill.

In a large mixing bowl, mix meats, egg, 2 TB Fisherman's Wharf Seasoning, 1/2 cup dried parsley, 1/2 cup fresh parmesan cheese, and chilled mushroom mix.

Take mixture and form 12 thin hamburger patties. Lay patties on dry wax paper. Take chilled cheeseball mix out of refrigerator and spoon 1/2 TB on half of the patties. Place plain patties on top of patties with cheeseball mix. Pinch the edges of both patties together, creating a closed hamburger pocket with the cheeseball mix in the middle. Cook burgers on grill until meat is cooked through.

SIDES: Serve burgers with sweet potato fries, grilled zucchini, and baby portabello mushrooms. *(See page 22 for additional side recipes.)*

Mango Salmon
with Mushroom Potatoes & Mango Basil Salad

Full of omega 3 fatty acids, salmon is one of the healthiest proteins you can eat!

This dish is rich in flavor and showcases the luxurious texture of the salmon by using citrus and mango notes throughout.

We've paired it with a fresh Mango Basil Salad and a Mushroom Potato Mash. Of course, if you are watching your carbs, our Sauteed Green Beans could be substituted for the potatoes.

All Ingredients
(serves 2)

- 2 Salmon Steak Fillets
- Mango Tequila Jalapeño Grill Sauce (By Earth & Vine)
- 2 Limes
- 1 Whole Garlic
- 2 TB Yogurt Butter (Brummel & Brown)
- 2 TB Olive Oil
- 2 Mangos
- Handful of Fresh Basil
- 2 Med. Size Russet Potatoes
- 2-3 cups Sliced Porcini Mushrooms
- Fisherman's Wharf Seasoning

MANGO BASIL SALAD

This dish is so simple and most of all, delicious! Simply dice 2 mangos into a bowl, then take a generous handful of basil and snip it into the mango using kitchen shears. Cut one of your limes and squeeze the juice over the mango and basil. Mix well and put into the refrigerator to chill.

This simple side dish can be prepared before you start anything else and will be ready to eat after 30 minutes in the refrigerator.

MUSHROOM POTATO MASH

In a large saucepan, boil filtered water, and add 1 TB olive oil. Chop potatoes and add to boiling water. While potatoes are cooking, add 1 TB yogurt butter to a medium saute pan over medium heat. Add 1 TB olive oil, diced garlic, and 2-3 cups sliced mushrooms. Saute mushrooms, and add 1 tsp of Fisherman's Wharf Seasoning. Saute until brown and set aside.

Drain cooked potatoes and place in a large mixing bowl. Roughly mash the potatoes. Add mushroom mixture to potatoes, mix, and set aside to plate with main course.

MANGO SALMON

In a medium saute pan, add 1 TB yogurt butter, 1 TB olive oil, and sliced garlic. Saute over medium heat. Lay in salmon fillets. Slice lime, and squeeze the juice from one-half over the fish.

Gently flip fish after 3-5 minutes, decreasing the heat to low. Slowly drizzle 2 TB of Mango Grill Sauce over the salmon and sauté for an additional minute. Turn heat off, and let the fish sit for 1 minute.

Place the salmon on the plate and take some of the sauce from the pan to drizzle over the fish and serve. *(Take extra sauce and drizzle over potatoes)*

Salmon is always a fantastic choice, especially for health reasons.

However, if you'd like to switch up the feel of the dish every now and then, this recipe also works well with halibut and other whitefish.

Artichoke Pesto Pasta
with Herb Chicken

This is a simple, one dish meal that really delivers! By using a fantastic, pre-made Artichoke Lemon Pesto Sauce, you are able to create flavors that taste like you've been in the kitchen all day!

When time and convenience are factors, you can use premium quality pre-made products that add that gourmet touch to a quick meal. Luckily, these days you can find pre made products that are both tasty and healthy for you!

Ingredients
(serves 2)
2 Chicken Breasts
Artichoke Lemon Pesto
1 Whole Garlic Bulb
2 Cups Porcini Mushrooms
Whole Wheat Pasta
Fisherman's Wharf Seasoning
Olive Oil
Yogurt Butter
(Brummel & Brown)
Dried Parsley

Fill a medium saucepan with filtered water and add 1 TB of olive oil and 1 TB of Fisherman's Wharf Seasoning. Bring to boil and add pasta. Cook for 10-15 minutes, or until pasta is al dente. Strain pasta and set aside.

While the pasta is cooking, add 1 TB of Brummel Butter to a medium sized frying pan on medium heat, and slice chicken breasts into bite-sized pieces. Add 1 TB of olive oil to the butter. Once the butter has melted, add 2 cloves of garlic, then add sliced Porcini Mushrooms, and top with Fisherman's Wharf Seasoning. Once the mushrooms have browned, add the chicken pieces to the pan and saute until cooked. Wait until the chicken is cooked through, then add 2 TB of the Artichoke Lemon Pesto to the mixture, and mix together.

Add hot chicken mixture to cooked pasta. Mix, then top with dried parsley and enjoy!

Black Olive Pesto Pasta

Talk about convenience! The ingredients in this dish are almost exactly the same as the recipe for "Artichoke Pesto Pasta". By simply changing the type of pesto dip we use for the sauce, we've created an entirely different dish!

Proving that you can keep your weekly menus varied, and yummy without an overflowing pantry!

Ingredients
(serves 2)
2 Chicken Breasts
Black Olive Pesto Dip
1 Whole Garlic Sliced
2 Cups Porcini Mushrooms
3-4 Roma Tomatoes
Whole Wheat Pasta
Fisherman's Wharf Seasoning
Olive Oil
Yogurt Butter
(Brummel & Brown)

Fill a medium saucepan with filtered water, add 1 TB of olive oil, and 1 TB of Fisherman's Wharf Seasoning. Bring to boil and add pasta. Cook for 10-15 minutes, or until pasta is al dente. Strain pasta and set aside.

While the pasta is cooking, add 1 TB of Brummel Butter to a medium sized frying pan on medium heat, and slice chicken breasts into bite-sized pieces. Add 1 TB of olive oil to the butter. Once the butter has melted, add 2 cloves of sliced garlic, then add sliced Porcini Mushrooms, and top with Fisherman's Wharf Seasoning. Once the mushrooms have browned, add the chicken pieces to the pan and saute until cooked. Wait until the chicken is cooked through, then add 2 TB of the Black Olive Pesto Dip to the mixture, and mix together.

Add hot chicken mixture to the pasta, and mix. Then top with chopped tomatoes and enjoy!

Black Olive Pesto Dip from Bella Cucina.

WHOLE WHEAT PASTA

Many of us have been trained to believe that starchy carbs, like pasta should be cut out of our diets if we want to be healthy. While this is true of traditional white pasta, a good quality whole wheat pasta has a much lower effect on blood sugar levels, and is a healthy addition to your diet. Other pastas made from brown rice and quinoa are also good options.

Artichoke Flank Steak

This time, we've used one of our favorite ingredients, Fisherman's Wharf Seasonings, to bring out the flavor in a hearty flank steak. Combined with the artichokes and mushrooms, this dish is sure to satisfy just about anyone.

A healthy way to incorporate a small portion of beef into your healthy lifestyle!

Ingredients
(serves 2)

1/2 lb Flank Steak
1 Whole Garlic
3 Cups Porcini Mushrooms
1 Jar Artichokes in Olive Oil
Fisherman's Wharf Seasoning
Yogurt Butter
(Brummel & Brown)
Olive Oil

In a large saute pan, melt 1 TB over medium heat and add 1 TB of olive oil. Toss in sliced whole garlic cloves and 3 cups of sliced mushrooms. Add 1 TB of Fisherman's Wharf Seasoning, mix well and cook for 2 minutes.

Remove flank steak from packaging and cut into 4 pieces. Pound meat to tenderize, and rinse.

Place steak into the pan with mushrooms, and saute 1 minute on each side. If the meat is looking dry, add a bit more olive oil. Then add artichokes, drained. Finish cooking on low heat until meat is cooked to your taste.

SIDES: Serve steak with double baked sweet potato and sauteed spinach. *(See page 22 for additional side recipes.)*

Shopping Guide & More Sides

Let's face it, hectic schedules and busy lives can lead to poor eating habits. We all know junk food is terrible for us, but we often feel trapped by cost and convenience.

Moreover, I've found that my clients will only stick to a meal plan, if they can make it in about 30 minutes or have the option to freeze the left overs.

My goal with this cookbook is to make eating healthy completely worry-free and easy.

That's why I've created simple recipes, that use a core group of ingredients in new and inventive ways. This also takes a little pressure off the wallet, because you don't have to spend a mint stocking your kitchen to test out the recipes in this book.

I've also found that the key to gourmet-tasting meals, that can be completed in about 30 minutes, is to use premium quality, pre-made seasonings, sauces, and marinades.

In this section, I will identify a few of my favorite products, that I use all the time to make "ordinary" meals "extraordinary"!

Urban Accents' Fisherman's Wharf Seasoning

Wind & Willow Spinach Artichoke Cheeseball & Appetizer Mix
Net Wt. .5 oz. (15 g)

Wind & Willow Garlic Herb Cheeseball & Appetizer Mix
Net Wt. 1.2 oz. (35 g)

Wind & Willow Cheeseball mixes are one of my favorite secret ingredients!

You are what You Eat!

It's true, everything we put in our bodies is actively effecting how feel and, of course, how we look!

That's why it's so important to use the best ingredients possible when creating your quick and easy meals.

The ingredients that I use in this book generally fall into two categories:

1) **Fresh:** Including produce and fresh meat.

2) **Premium Pre-made:** All of the amazing marinades, mixes, and seasonings.

First, it's essential to cook with fresh produce as much as you can, in order to add vitamins and minerals that are often lost, if you choose preserved options like canned vegetables.

By using fresh produce and meat you will up the nutritional value of your food, and your dishes will always taste incredible too!

Secondly, I have hand-picked my favorite pre-made products, that I discovered at **Villa Cucina** in San Clemente, California. It

Christina from Villa Cucina and me.

was there that I was introduced to some of the most amazing pre-made products that I have ever tasted. Not only are they full of flavor, but they are made with the best ingredients and without many of the fillers and preservatives found in other products.

PRE-MADE INGREDIENT GUIDE

FISHERMAN'S WHARF SEASONING *by Urban Accents*
This diverse seasoning mix was originally intended for use with seafood and really helps to compliment the flavor of our salmon dish. This isn't just for seafood though! I've found it to be a wonderful addition to just about any dish that you're looking to add a deeper flavor to.

MANGO TEQUILA JALAPEÑO GRILLING & DIPPING SAUCE *by Earth & Vine*
Wow, what a versatile ingredient to have in your pantry! This sauce can be used as a marinade, a grilling sauce, or even a dipping sauce right out of the bottle. Incredible flavors, and unlimited ways to use it!

BLACK OLIVE PESTO *by Bella Cucina*
Most traditional pestos don't include black olives, but in this unique pre-made product the makers were able to successfully combine the flavor of traditional pesto with hints of a olive tapenade. Truly unique flavor that will make your recipes stand out.

ARTICHOKE PESTO *by Elki*
Artichokes add so much personality to any dish, but many who aren't comfortable with artichokes, can often be intimidated on how to use them effectively in their cooking. This product makes it easy to create gourmet flavor fast without the expertise.

GARLIC HERB CHEESEBALL & APPETIZER MIX *by Wind & Willow*
Who would have thought a cheeseball mix would be the perfect secret ingredient to a burger? This mix truly is one of my secrets to incredible burgers that keep my friends an family asking for more! The mix can also be used to make dips and appetizers.

If you have difficulty finding these products in your local shop, please check out my favorite home and kitchen store, Villa Cucina, on the web. They would be happy to supply these ingredients via mail order.

www.villacucina.com

Other specialized ingredients that you'll need for this book include:

YOGURT BUTTER *by Brummel & Brown*

SESAME GINGER DRESSING LITE *by Newman's Own*

LITE SOY SAUCE *any brand*

DOUBLE BAKED SWEET POTATO

2 Sweet Potatoes
Yogurt Butter
(Brummel & Brown)
2 tsp Cinnamon

Choose 2 sweet potatoes medium sized, sufficient for a personal serving. Rinse sweet potoato, and perforate with a fork or knife.

Microwave for 3 minutes, and let cool for 2 minutes. Microwave for another 2 minutes. Then slice potato lengthwise, and score each half. Blend in yogurt butter. Microwave for 2 more minutes.

Then blend in cinnamon.
(Optional)

SAUTEED GREEN BEANS

2 cups Fresh Green Beans
1 tsp Fisherman's Wharf
3 Garlic Cloves
1/4 Cup Toasted Slivered Almonds
Yogurt Butter
(Brummel & Brown)

In medium sized saucepan melt 1 TB of yogurt butter. Toss in sliced garlic, and saute for a minute or two. Add Fisherman's Wharf Seasoning, and stir thoroughly.

Add cleaned green beans to pan, and continually stir for 5 minutes, for al dente cooked beans.

Once beans are cooked to your preference, add toasted slivered almonds and toss.

SWEET POTATO FRIES

2 Sweet Potatoes
Yogurt Butter
(Brummel & Brown)
2 tsp Cinnamon
Blue Agave Syrup

Clean and peel sweet potatoes. Slice potatoes into circles, and julienne the precut circles into fry shapes.

Rinse fries in water. Then in a medium sized saucepan melt 1 TB of yogurt butter. Add fries to butter and continually stir over medium heat. *(Add more butter if fries become dry)*

After fries begin to soften *(5-10 minutes)*, dust in cinnamon. Continue to heat over medium heat until fries are completely cooked.

Add 1 TB Agave Syrup, and stir. *(Optional)*

GRILLED ZUCCHINI

3-4 Zucchini
1 tsp Fisherman's Wharf Yogurt Butter
(Brummel & Brown)

Rinse zucchini, and remove ends. Cut zucchini in half, and quarter each half.

In a medium sized saute pan melt butter over medium heat, and add zucchini. Saute for 2 minutes. Then dust in Fisherman's Wharf Seasoning, stirring until zucchini is thoroughly cooked.

To cook on a grill, simply put all ingredients into a tin foil envelope, and grill until cooked.

BABY PORTABELLOS

4 Baby Portabellos
1 tsp Fisherman's Wharf Yogurt Butter
(Brummel & Brown)

Rinse and clean mushrooms.

In a medium sized saute pan melt butter over medium heat. Add mushrooms and saute for 2 minutes each side.

Dust in Fisherman's Wharf Seasoning, and continue cooking for another minute.

To cook on a grill, simply put all ingredients into a tin foil envelope, and grill until cooked.

SAUTEED SPINACH

1 Bag Baby Spinach
3-4 Garlic Cloves
1 tsp Fisherman's Wharf Yogurt Butter
(Brummel & Brown)

Rinse spinach, and snip off ends.

In a medium sized saucepan melt 1 TB butter over medium heat. Add sliced garlic and saute for 1-2 minutes. Dust in Fisherman's Wharf Seasoning, and stir.

Add rinsed spinach and saute until spinach is thoroughly cooked.

Brummel & Brown Yogurt Butter can be substituted with olive oil, or 1/2 tsp of butter with 1/2 tsp of olive oil for additional flavor if desired.

Thank you, Mom and Dad, for letting me be me, and setting a great example in life!

A sincere thank you to my high school friend, Robert Lyn Nelson. This would not have been possible without you.

Thanks to Randy Robertson for my logo.

Also, a special thanks to Leah Latini. Without your help and creativity, it would never have been. You are amazing. This book is everything I hoped for, and without you, I would have been lost!

www.ingramcontent.com/pod-product-compliance
Lightning Source LLC
Chambersburg PA
CBHW042020150426
43197CB00002B/83